IT'S TIME TO EAT PEPPERONI PIZZA

It's Time to Eat PEPPERONI PIZZA

Walter the Educator

Silent King Books
A WhichHead Entertainment Imprint

Copyright © 2025 by Walter the Educator

All rights reserved. No part of this book may be reproduced in any manner whatsoever without written per- mission except in the case of brief quotations embodied in critical articles and reviews.

First Printing, 2024

Disclaimer

This book is a literary work; the story is not about specific persons, locations, situations, and/or circumstances unless mentioned in a historical context. Any resemblance to real persons, locations, situations, and/or circumstances is coincidental. This book is for entertainment and informational purposes only. The author and publisher offer this information without warranties expressed or implied. No matter the grounds, neither the author nor the publisher will be accountable for any losses, injuries, or other damages caused by the reader's use of this book. The use of this book acknowledges an understanding and acceptance of this disclaimer.

It's Time to Eat PEPPERONI PIZZA is a collectible early learning book by Walter the Educator suitable for all ages belonging to Walter the Educator's Time to Eat Book Series. Collect more books at WaltertheEducator.com

USE THE EXTRA SPACE TO TAKE NOTES AND DOCUMENT YOUR MEMORIES

PEPPERONI PIZZA

It's dinner time, oh what a treat,

It's Time to Eat
Pepperoni Pizza

Something cheesy, warm, and neat!

On my plate, just take a peek,

Pepperoni pizza, yum to eat!

Golden crust, so crisp and round,

Melty cheese all soft and brown.

Pepperoni, red and bright,

Oh, this smells just right tonight!

Take a slice and lift it high,

Cheese goes stretching to the sky!

One big bite and then I grin,

Pepperoni fun begins!

Saucy, cheesy, full of zest,

Every bite is just the best.

Crunchy, chewy, spicy, too,

I could eat a slice, or two!

It's Time to Eat Pepperoni Pizza

Mom and Dad both grab a plate,

Sister says, "I just can't wait!"

Brother takes a giant slice,

Then he takes another bite!

Dip in ranch or eat it plain,

Either way, it's all the same.

Tasty, yummy, super great,

Pepperoni's worth the wait!

Oh no! My slice is nearly gone,

I've been munching way too long!

Just one more? I smile and say,

Maybe save some for the day?

Pizza party, what a blast,

Eating slow or eating fast!

Stacking slices way up high,

It's Time to Eat
Pepperoni Pizza

Pepperoni pizza pie!

Now my tummy's feeling tight,

Every bite was such delight!

Full and happy, now I know,

Pizza makes my heart just glow!

Time for bed, the night is near,

But one more thought is crystal clear,

Tomorrow's meal? Oh yes, indeed,

It's Time to Eat
Pepperoni Pizza

More pepperoni's what I need!

ABOUT THE CREATOR

Walter the Educator is one of the pseudonyms for Walter Anderson. Formally educated in Chemistry, Business, and Education, he is an educator, an author, a diverse entrepreneur, and he is the son of a disabled war veteran. "Walter the Educator" shares his time between educating and creating. He holds interests and owns several creative projects that entertain, enlighten, enhance, and educate, hoping to inspire and motivate you. Follow, find new works, and stay up to date with Walter the Educator™

at WaltertheEducator.com

www.ingramcontent.com/pod-product-compliance
Lightning Source LLC
LaVergne TN
LVHW052014060526
838201LV00059B/4021